Introduction

'The principal focus in lower key stage 2 is to ensure that pupils become increasingly fluent with whole numbers, including number facts ... and develop efficient mental methods to perform calculations accurately.'

Lower Key Stage 2 National Curriculum Programme of Study

'The teacher created a positive climate for learning in which pupils were interested and engaged.'

OFSTED Inspector

Welcome to a world of mathematical fun and games!

Easy to play and requiring only basic equipment, these educational games engage even the most reluctant of learners whilst boosting confidence for all.

Great for teachers, intervention workers, teaching assistants, private tutors and parents, the flexible nature of this game pack offers:

▶ practice for specific objectives from the new National Curriculum

▶ a great resource to:
"ensure students are engaged in learning and generate high levels of commitment to learning"
(Outstanding Grade Descriptors, *Ofsted School Inspection Handbook* (updated 2014))

▶ the opportunity to demonstrate a commitment to:
"*the social development of pupils at the school*" within curriculum time
(Ofsted Framework for School Inspection (updated 2014))

▶ an effective assessment tool

▶ the promotion of problem solving and thinking skills through game strategy

▶ fun homework activities

Playing Information

All these games require a pack of playing cards and most also need some kind of coloured counters or other objects such as beads or buttons. Suitable materials are available from Tarquin - see page 40 for details. When the picture cards are used the jack represents number eleven, the queen is number twelve and the king is thirteen. To help children remember this you may want to consider writing the actual numbers in the corners of each card.

And that's all you need to know to enjoy years of happy gaming!

David Smith

Hexums

Focus

Hexums is a game for two or three players which practices recall of facts for the 3, 4 and 8 multiplication tables.

What you need

▶ Playing cards (kings removed)
▶ Counters (a different colour for each player)
▶ Hexums game board

How to play

When the kings have been removed from the pack the remaining cards are shuffled and placed in a pile, face-down and within reach of all the players. Player 1 turns over a playing card from the pack and places it face-up in front of them. The number on the card is then multiplied: by three if playing Hexums 3, by four in Hexums 4, and by eight in Hexums 8.

For example

Player 1 turns over a six so must say 6 x 3 = 18. After saying the correct answer Player 1 can place a counter on any of the matching answers on the game board.

Player 2 then turns over a card and multiplies the number by three. This time a queen is turned over so Player 2 says 12 x 3 = 36 and can also place a counter on any of the matching answers on the game board.

Players continue to take cards in turn, multiply the number on the card and place their counters on the board. If a player gives an incorrect answer they are not able to place a counter on that turn.

How to win

Each player has to try and make a continuous line of coloured counters on adjacent numbers from the outer ring to the inner ring of shaded hexagons, as shown in the diagram.

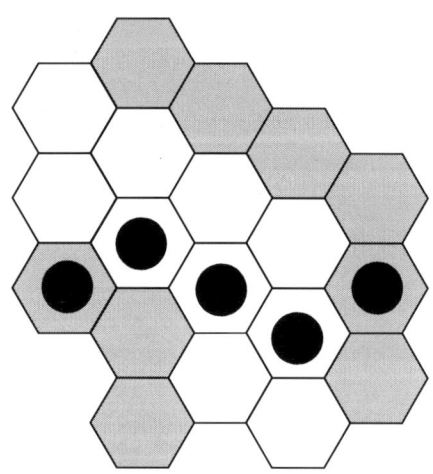

Rule changes / Next steps

▶ Limit the players to twelve counters each to try and get a winner.
▶ Record multiplication facts on paper or a whiteboard. At the end of the game use these to generate other multiplication and division facts (as below) and then test each other.

6 x 3 = 18	so	18 = 3 x 6	18 ÷ 3 = 6	3 = 18 ÷ 6
12 x 3 = 36	so	36 = 3 x 12	36 ÷ 3 = 12	3 = 36 ÷ 12

ACE Mathematics Games 3

13 exciting blackline activities to engage ages 7 — 8
David Smith

3. **Introduction**

4. **Hexums**
   recall facts for the
   3, 4 and 8 multiplication tables

8. **Square Up**
   recall facts for the
   3, 4 and 8 multiplication tables

12. **Flamingo Bingo**
    fluent recall and use of
    addition and subtraction facts to 20

16. **Cover Up**
    fluent recall and use of
    addition and subtraction facts to 20

18. **Get Rid**
    add and subtract one and two-digit
    numbers up to 30

19. **Hooked!**
    add and subtract one and two-digit
    numbers up to 80

22. **Battle Squares**
    add and subtract two-digit numbers
    up to 100

25. **Dare!**
    add and subtract two-digit numbers
    up to 100

28. **Speed Seekers**
    add and subtract two-digit numbers
    with some numbers exceeding 100

31. **The Thousand Dash**
    add and subtract three-digit numbers and tens
    with numbers up to 1000

33. **Tower Power**
    use a range of efficient mental methods
    with numbers up to 20

34. **Trios**
    use a range of efficient mental methods with
    numbers up to 100

36. **Monster Mash-Up!**
    use a range of efficient mental methods with
    numbers up to 1000

Acknowledgements

Thanks are due to many people but especially to my lovely wife and also my dear mum who between them patiently played all the games with me to test their initial suitability. I also have to thank the teachers and children of Peel Park Primary School for giving them a road test, spotting my errors and making suggestions on how they could be further developed and improved. Finally thanks go to the staff at Tarquin, for their support in the editing process.

Dedication

This book is dedicated to the memory of Maxine Firth, an inspirational friend and colleague who shared my ideal of an enjoyment of mathematics for all.

Published by Tarquin Publications
Suite 74, 17 Holywell Hill
St Albans
AL1 1DT

www.tarquingroup.com

Copyright © David Smith, 2014
ISBN: 978-1-907-55093-5

Distributed in the USA by IPG Books
www.ipgbook.com
www.amazon.com & major retailers

Distributed in Australia by OLM www.lat-olm.com.au

All rights reserved. Sheets may be copied singly for use by the purchaser only, or for class use under a valid school or institutional licence from the relevant Copyright Licensing society.

Printed and bound by CPI Group (UK) Ltd, Croydon, CR0 4YY

Hexums x 3

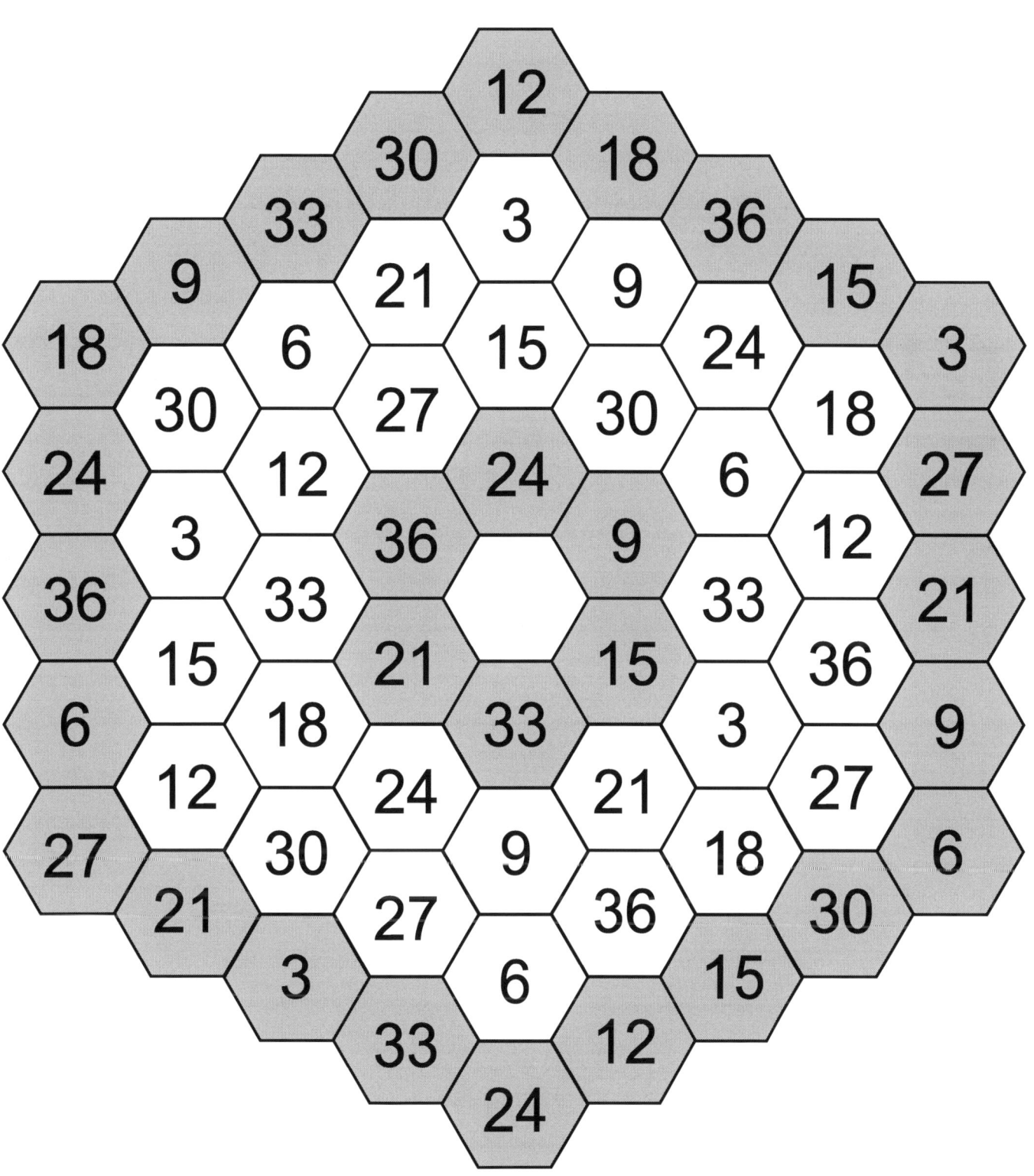

Hexums x 4

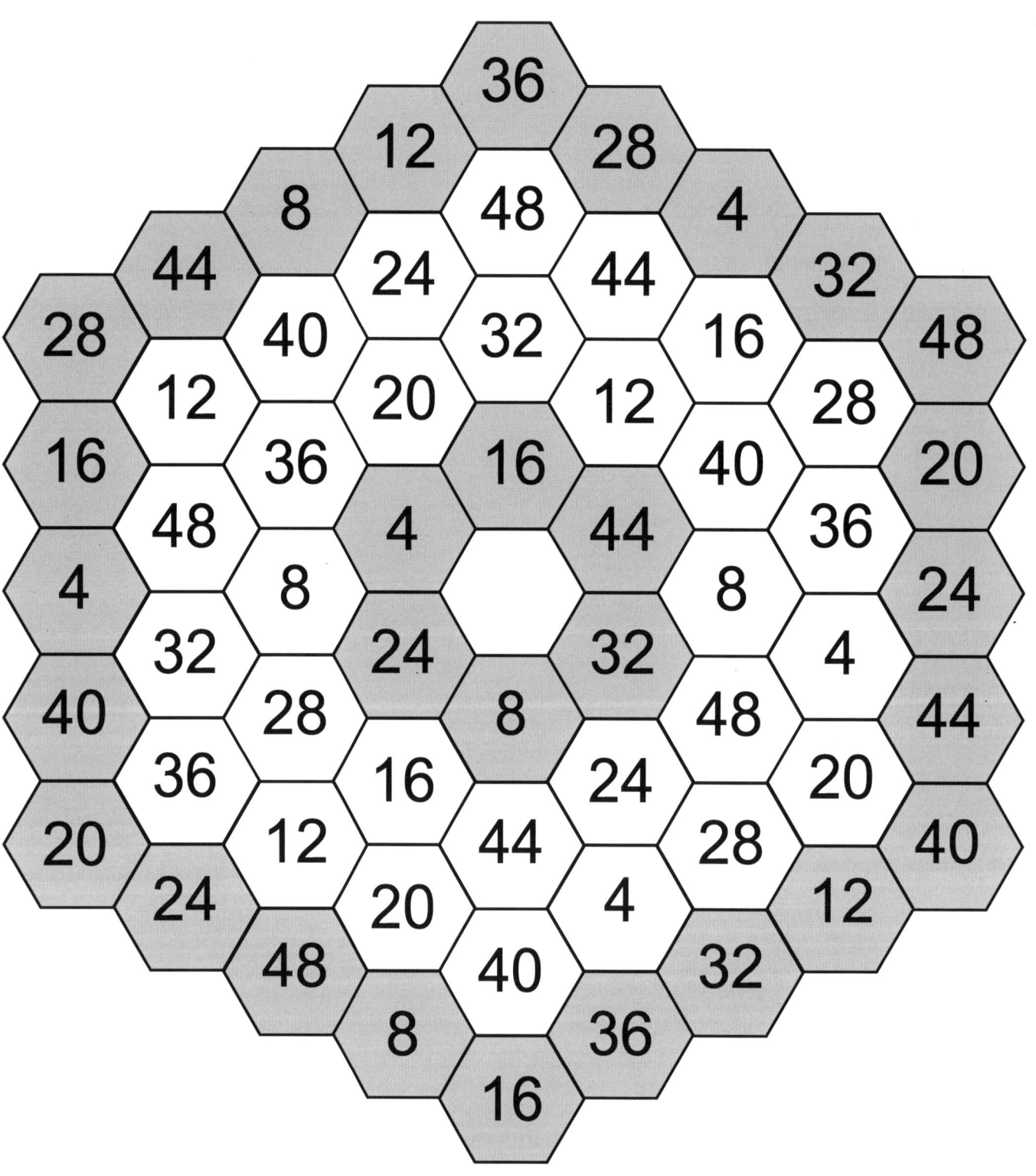

Hexums x 8

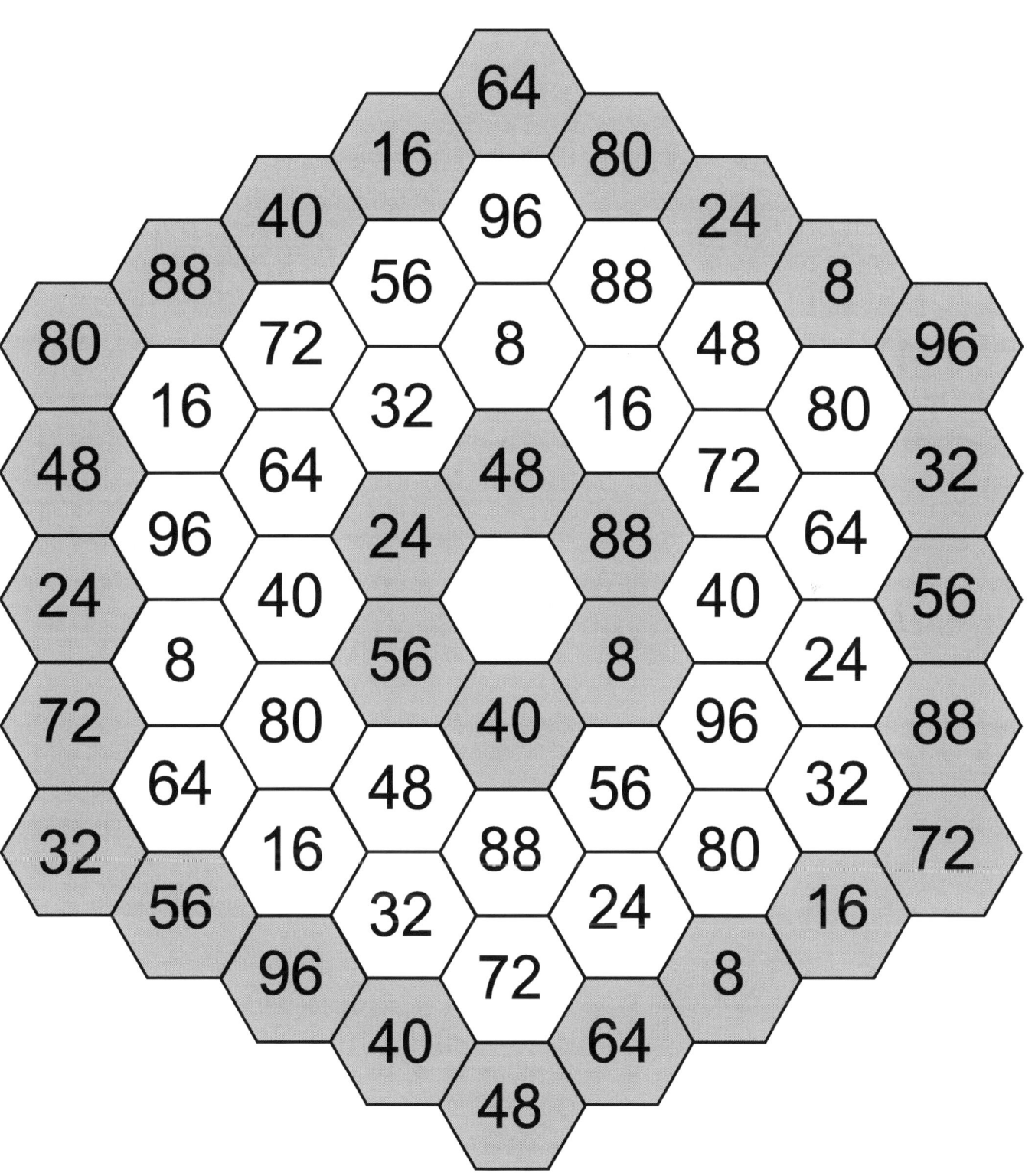

Game Board © Tarquin Photocopiable under licence – for terms see page 2

Square Up

Focus

Square Up is a game for two to four players which practices recall of multiplication facts for the 3, 4 and 8 multiplication tables.

What you need

▶ Playing cards (kings removed)
▶ Counters (a different colour for each player)
▶ Square Up game board

How to play

When the kings have been removed from the pack the remaining cards are shuffled and placed in a pile, face-down and within reach of all the players. Player 1 turns over a playing card from the pack and places it face-up in front of them. The card is then multiplied: by three if playing Square Up 3, by four in Square Up 4, and by eight in Square Up 8.

For example (Square Up 4)

Player 1 turns over an eight so must say 8 x 4 = 32. After saying the correct answer Player 1 can place a counter on any of the matching answers on the game board.

Player 2 then turns over a card and multiplies the number by four. This time a jack is turned over so Player 2 says 11 x 4 = 44 and can also place a counter on any of the matching answers on the game board.

Players continue to take cards in turn, multiply the number on the card and place their counters on the board. If a player gives an incorrect answer they are not able to place a counter on that turn. A player may turn over another card if no matching answer can be found on the game board.

How to win

Players have to make the shape of a square, by placing counters on each corner, as shown in the diagram. The square can be any size and the first player to complete one is the winner.

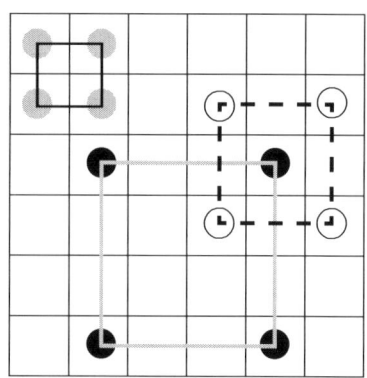

Rule changes / Next steps

▶ Players score four points for each square they make and play can continue until all their counters have been used or until there are no spaces left on the game board.

▶ Make some flashcards showing the multiplication or division facts on one side and the answer on the other side. Children can then use them for individual practice or to test a partner.

SQUARE UP 3

18	30	12	3	24	15
33	24	6	9	21	30
27	36	15	18	3	6
3	21	30	12	27	33
15	9	33	24	36	21
36	12	18	6	9	27

 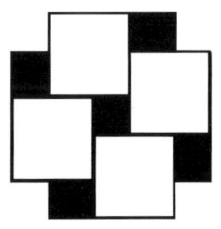

SQUARE UP 4

28	44	20	36	12	4
4	16	8	32	44	48
48	20	40	24	28	16
12	8	36	4	40	32
40	24	28	12	48	20
32	16	44	8	24	36

SQUARE UP 8

56	48	88	80	32	96
64	96	24	16	48	8
16	40	8	32	72	56
72	80	64	88	40	24
96	24	48	56	16	88
40	32	72	8	80	64

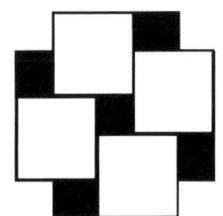 

Flamingo Bingo

Focus

Flamingo Bingo is a game for two or more players which practices fluent recall and use of addition and subtraction facts to twenty.

What you need

▶ Playing cards
▶ Counters
▶ Flamingo Bingo cards
▶ Whiteboard / paper and pen

How to play

Each player needs to start the game with a Flamingo Bingo card, eight counters and a whiteboard or paper and pen. The cards are shuffled and placed in a pile, face-down and within reach of all the players. Player 1 starts the game by turning over three cards. All players then use these three numbers in different ways, using only addition and subtraction, to try and make a number on their game card.

For example

Player 1 turns over a four, a two and a seven. Different numbers can be made as follows:

4 + 2 = 6	7 − 2 = 5	7 − 4 = 3
7 + 4 + 2 = 13	7 − 4 − 2 = 1	7 + 4 − 2 = 9
24 − 7 = 17	4 − 2 = 2	4 + 7 = 11

Players need to write down their calculation on paper or a whiteboard to show how they made the number on their bingo card and then cover it with a counter. A time limit of ten, twenty or thirty seconds needs to be placed on players to make a number. A player can only place one counter for each round. If a player can't think of a way to make an uncovered number, they can't place a counter for that round.

Play continues with players taking turns to put three cards face-up for all players to try and make another number on their card.

How to win

Players have to achieve a 'full house' by covering every number on their card. The first player to stand on one leg and shout 'Flamingo Bingo' (not compulsory!) is the winner. Players' calculations are checked at the end of the game to make sure they are correct.

Rule changes / Next steps

▶ Have one player as a referee who turns over cards and checks answers. Play as a whole class by having one bingo card between two or use the spare cards to make one each.

▶ Turn over four or five cards and give the players five minutes to try and make all the numbers on their bingo card by using only this one set of numbers. Children could be allowed to use multiplication and division as well as addition and subtraction.

Flamingo Bingo Cards © Tarquin Photocopiable under licence – for terms see page 2

Cover Up

Focus

Cover Up is a game for two to four players which practices fluent recall and use of addition and subtraction facts to twenty.

What you need

▶ Playing cards (picture cards removed)

▶ Counters

▶ Cover Up game board

How to play

The picture cards are removed from the pack. The cards are shuffled, three cards are dealt to each player and the remaining cards are placed in a pile, face-down and within reach of all the players. Players must then look at their cards and try to find ways of making one of the numbers on their row. Player 1 goes first and must place two or three cards face-up in front of them to match a number on their row.

For example
Player 1 puts down different combinations of these cards to make any of the following possible numbers:

8 + 3 = 11   8 − 3 = 5   8 + 2 + 3 = 13   8 + 3 − 2 = 9

8 + 2 − 3 = 7   23 − 8 = 15   8 − 3 − 2 = 3

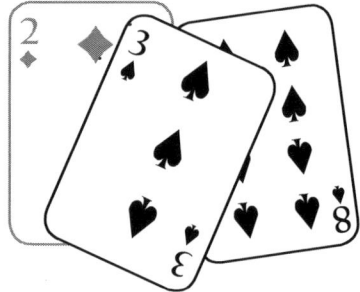

The other players must check that the calculation is correct, and if so Player 1 can place a counter onto the number on their row. Player 1 then picks up two or three more cards from the top of the pack to replace the cards they used. Play continues with players taking it in turns to put cards down to try and make different answers.

Only one number can be covered with a counter on each turn. If a player can't make a number on their row they can choose to change one, two or all three of their cards instead. They place the cards they don't want on the bottom of the central pile and take the same number of new cards from the top. However, this exchange of cards counts as the player's turn: they are not allowed to try to place a counter. When the cards in the middle run out the next player picks up all those in front of each player, shuffles them and places them back face-down in a pile again.

How to win

The first player to cover all the numbers on their row with a counter is the winner.

Rule changes / Next steps

▶ If a player puts down two cards of the same value (two fours or two sevens) when making an answer they can perform a 'double' trick. This means that as well as placing a counter on their own Cover Up number row they can also remove any one counter from another player's row. Using three of the same card could count as a 'triple trick' enabling the player to place one of their own counters and remove two from any opponent or one each from two different opponents.

▶ Investigate adding and subtracting different combinations of odd and even numbers.

Instruction Sheet © Tarquin Photocopiable under licence – for terms see page 2

COVER UP

Game Board © Tarquin Photocopiable under licence – for terms see page 2

Get Rid!

Focus

Get Rid is a game for two or more players which practices adding and subtracting one and two-digit numbers up to thirty.

What you need

▶ Playing cards

▶ Whiteboard / paper and pen

How to play

Before play can begin, Get Rid numbers must be chosen by the players. Player 1 can be asked to pick a random number between ten and twenty and Player 2 another between twenty and thirty. In this example the numbers chosen are twelve and twenty-seven. After shuffling the cards Player 1 deals out five to each player and places the rest of the pack face-down and within reach of all the players.

Players must then look at their cards and try to find out how they can add or subtract to make a total of either twelve or twenty-seven. As Player 1 dealt the cards, Player 2 goes first and must pick up a card from the top of the central pile to start their turn. They then see if they can use any of their cards to make either of the Get Rid numbers. Players can use addition and subtraction of several numbers, and have the option of putting two cards together to make a two-digit number.

For example

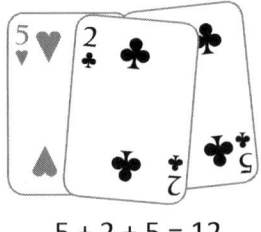      

5 + 2 + 5 = 12   18 − 6 = 12   37 − 10 = 27

If they can find a set, the cards are placed down for other players to see and check that they are correct. If they can't find a set of cards to make either of the Get Rid numbers they must wait to pick up another card on their next turn. Play continues with players picking up cards in turn and trying to make Get Rid numbers. Players score 8 points for each set of cards making the higher Get Rid number and 4 points for a set making the lower number.

A round lasts until one of the players 'Gets Rid' of all of their cards. If no player is able to use all their cards in this way then the round ends when all the cards in the pile have been used. The player who puts down all their cards receives a Get Rid bonus of 10 points. All the other players have to take away 2 points for each card they still have left in their hand.

Record the scores for the round using a whiteboard or paper and pen and then play again. Set different Get Rid numbers for the next round.

How to win

The winner is the player with the most points after an agreed number of rounds.

Rule changes / Next steps

▶ Allow players to use multiplication and division as well as addition and subtraction.

Hooked!

Focus

Hooked! is a game for two players which practices adding and subtracting one and two-digit numbers up to eighty.

What you need

▶ Playing cards

▶ Counter

▶ Hooked! game board

How to play

The cards are shuffled and placed in a pile, face-down between both players. Decide who is counting forwards and who is counting backwards. The player counting forwards moves from left to right along the game board and the player counting backwards moves from right to left. Place a counter on the middle number of the game board.

Players take it in turns to turn over a card and that number is added to or subtracted from (depending on the player's direction of play) the number underneath the counter.

For example

Player 1 (adding) turns over a six. They say 25 + 6 = 31 and then move to that square on the game board. Player 2 (subtracting) then turns an eight. They say 31 – 8 = 23 and move the counter to that square.

Players must perform the mental calculation before moving the counter, and a correct answer must be given in order to move. When all the cards have been used, shuffle them and place them back down in a pile so that play can continue.

How to win

Player 2 (subtracting) hooks the fish and wins by getting the counter to land on or go past zero whilst Player 1 (adding) hooks the fish and wins by getting the counter to land on or go past fifty (or eighty if playing Hooked! 80).

Rule changes / Next steps

▶ Change characters and play again so both players practice their addition and subtraction skills.

▶ Play for a set number of turns and the player who is closest to their end of the game board wins.

▶ For Hooked! 80 players turn over a card and **must double its value** before adding or subtracting this amount to the number underneath the counter.

▶ Allow players to do the calculation by counting up or down whilst moving the counter.

▶ Encourage children to investigate patterns in adding and subtracting numbers, such as
25 + 6 = 31   35 + 6 = 41   45 + 6 = 51   **so**   55 + 6 = ___   and so on.

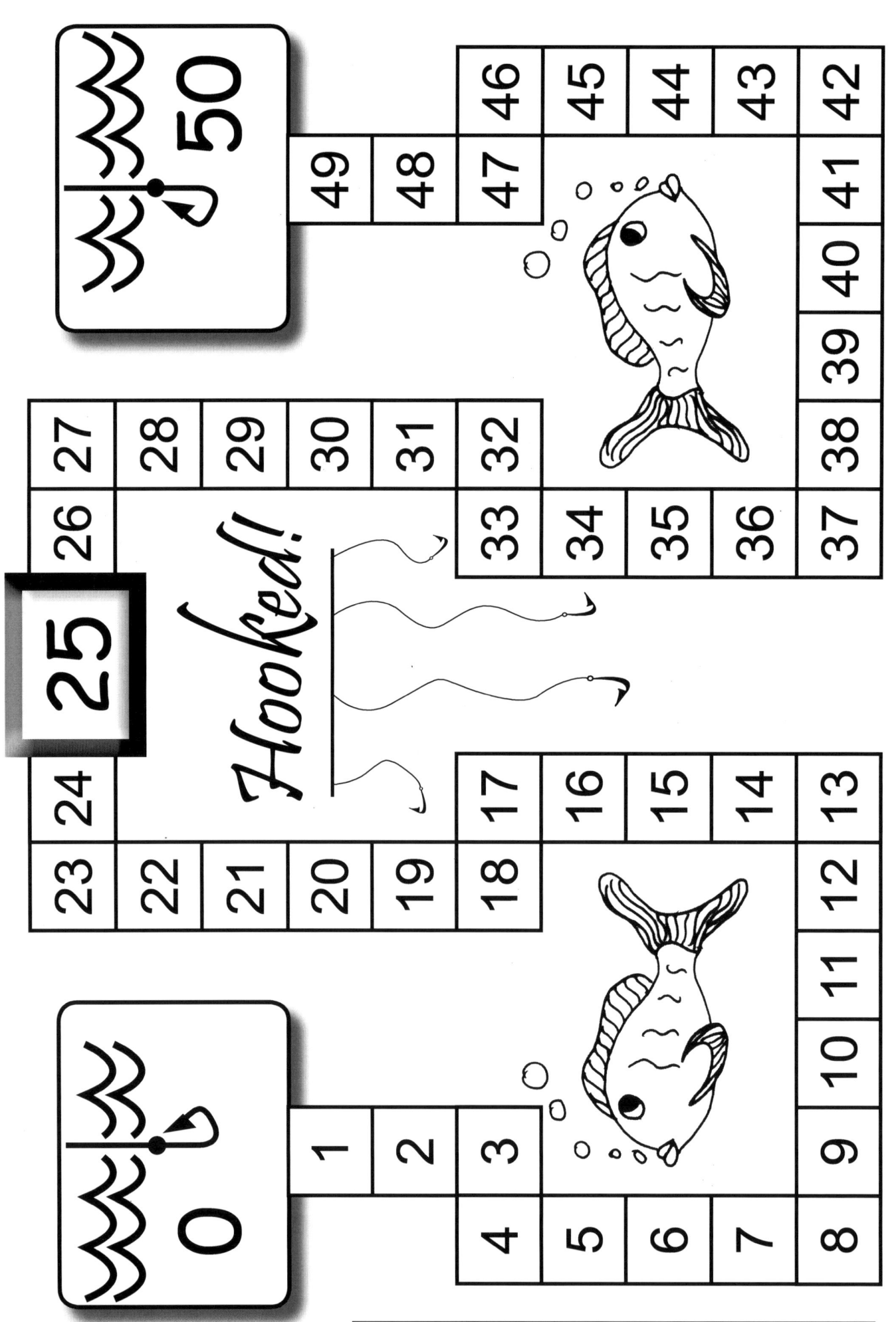

Hooked!

Battle Squares

Focus
Battle Squares is a game for two or more players which practices adding and subtracting two-digit numbers up to one hundred.

What you need
▶ Playing cards (tens and picture cards removed)
▶ Counters (a different colour for each player)
▶ Battle Squares game board
▶ Battle Squares scorecard

How to play

When the tens and picture cards have been removed from the pack the remaining cards are shuffled and placed in a pile, face-down and within reach of all the players.

Player 1 turns over two cards and uses them to make a two-digit number.

For example
If Player 1 turns over a 3 and a 7 they can either make the number 37 or 73. They must calculate how much more needs to be added to each two-digit number to make one hundred, and then decide which of their two-digit number options will get them the most points.

Player 1 may decide to calculate 37 + 63 = 100 and put a counter on sixty-three to score five points for a black square. However, if Player 1 decided to calculate 73 + 27 = 100 and put a counter on twenty-seven, they would score ten points for a grey square.

Play continues with players taking it in turns to make two-digit numbers and calculating how many more to make one hundred. They then decide where to place their counters on the board to score the maximum number of points possible (players should watch out for dotty squares, which lose them points). Each player keeps their own score using a scorecard. Players must do all their mental calculations before placing their counter and must also give a correct answer in order to do so.

If a square is already covered by a counter then the player must switch their cards around to make a different two-digit number and must place their counter on the other available square. If both possible squares are covered then the player cannot place a counter but draws two new cards on their next turn. When all the cards have been used, shuffle them and place them in a pile, face-down, ready for the next player's turn.

How to win
The winner of the battle is the player with the most points after an agreed number of rounds.

Rule changes / Next steps
▶ Do calculations as subtraction from one hundred, such as 100 − 54 = 46 or 100 − 45 = 55.
▶ Players turn over three cards and can use any combination of them to make a two-digit number.
▶ Change the number of points gained for each colour to practice adding different amounts when keeping score.
▶ Play "in colour": a full colour downloadable game board and scorecards are available on our website, www.tarquingroup.com.

BATTLE SQUARES

1	2	3	4	5	6	7	8	9	
11	12	13	14	15	16	17	18	19	S
21	22	23	24	25	26	27	28	29	Q
31	32	33	34	35	36	37	38	39	U
41	42	43	44	45	46	47	48	49	A
51	52	53	54	55	56	57	58	59	R
61	62	63	64	65	66	67	68	69	E
71	72	73	74	75	76	77	78	79	S
81	82	83	84	85	86	87	88	89	
	B	A	T	T	L	E			100

Full colour game board and scorecards downloadable from www.tarquingroup.com.

BATTLE SQUARES SCORECARD

□ = 2 points   ■ = 5 points   ▦ = 20 points

▨ = 10 points   ▧ = -9 points

Keep your score like this:

Round Number	Points for square	Total Game points
1	stripes, 20 points	20
2	dotty, -9	20 - 9 = 11
3	grey, 10	11 + 10 = 21

Round Number	Points for square	Total Game points
1		
2		
3		
4		
5		
6		
7		
8		
9		
10		
11		
12		
13		
14		
15		

Dare!

Focus

Dare is a game for two or more players which practices adding and subtracting one and two-digit numbers up to one hundred.

What you need

▶ Playing cards

▶ Counters (a different colour for each player)

▶ Dare! game board

How to play

Firstly, the cards are shuffled and placed in a pile, face-down and within reach of all the players.

Player 1 takes a card and then subtracts this number from a hundred, moving their counter to the relevant number on the game board.

Player 1 must then decide whether to play safe, stop and pass the cards to the next player or to 'dare' and turn over another card. If Player 1 decides to dare and turn over another card then:

▶ if the card is the same colour they can continue by subtracting the value of the card from the number underneath their counter;

▶ if the card is a different colour they must go back to the first grey **DARE SQUARE** they reach by moving backwards along the game board.

If Player 1 decides to stop then play goes to Player 2. Play continues with players taking cards in turn and subtracting the value of the card from the number underneath their counter on the game board.

Players must do all their mental calculations before moving their counter. The player must also give a correct answer to move their counter otherwise it remains in the same place on the game board.

If a player lands on top of another counter, the counter landed on is moved back to the start or the first **DARE SQUARE** they reach by moving backwards along the game board (whichever is agreed by the players before play).

How to win

The first player to land on or go past zero (the finish line) on the game board is the winner.

Rule changes / Next steps

▶ For Dare! 100 players turn over a card and must double this number before subtracting the total from the number underneath the counter. Take the lower number cards (1–4) out of the pack to make players subtract more of the larger numbers.

▶ Play as an addition game, starting at zero and adding up to the finish line.

▶ Each player starts with a blue dare counter and is allowed to use it once at any time during the game. The dare counter forces another player to dare and carry on even when they have decided to stop. The dared player must then carry on for two more cards. The same rules apply as outlined previously. However, if they turn over a card of a different colour they must go back to the first **DARE SQUARE** they reach by moving backwards from where they started that turn.

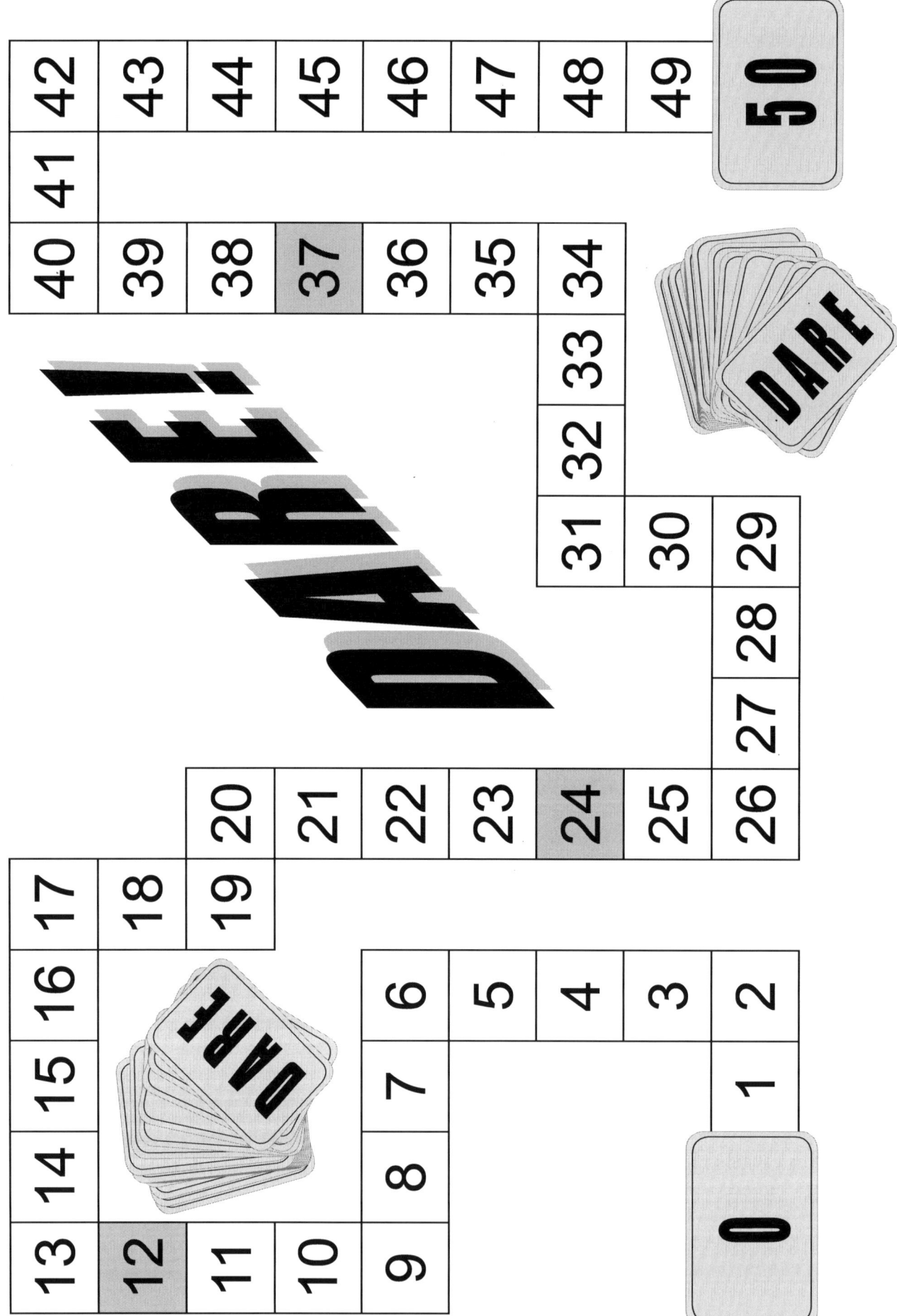

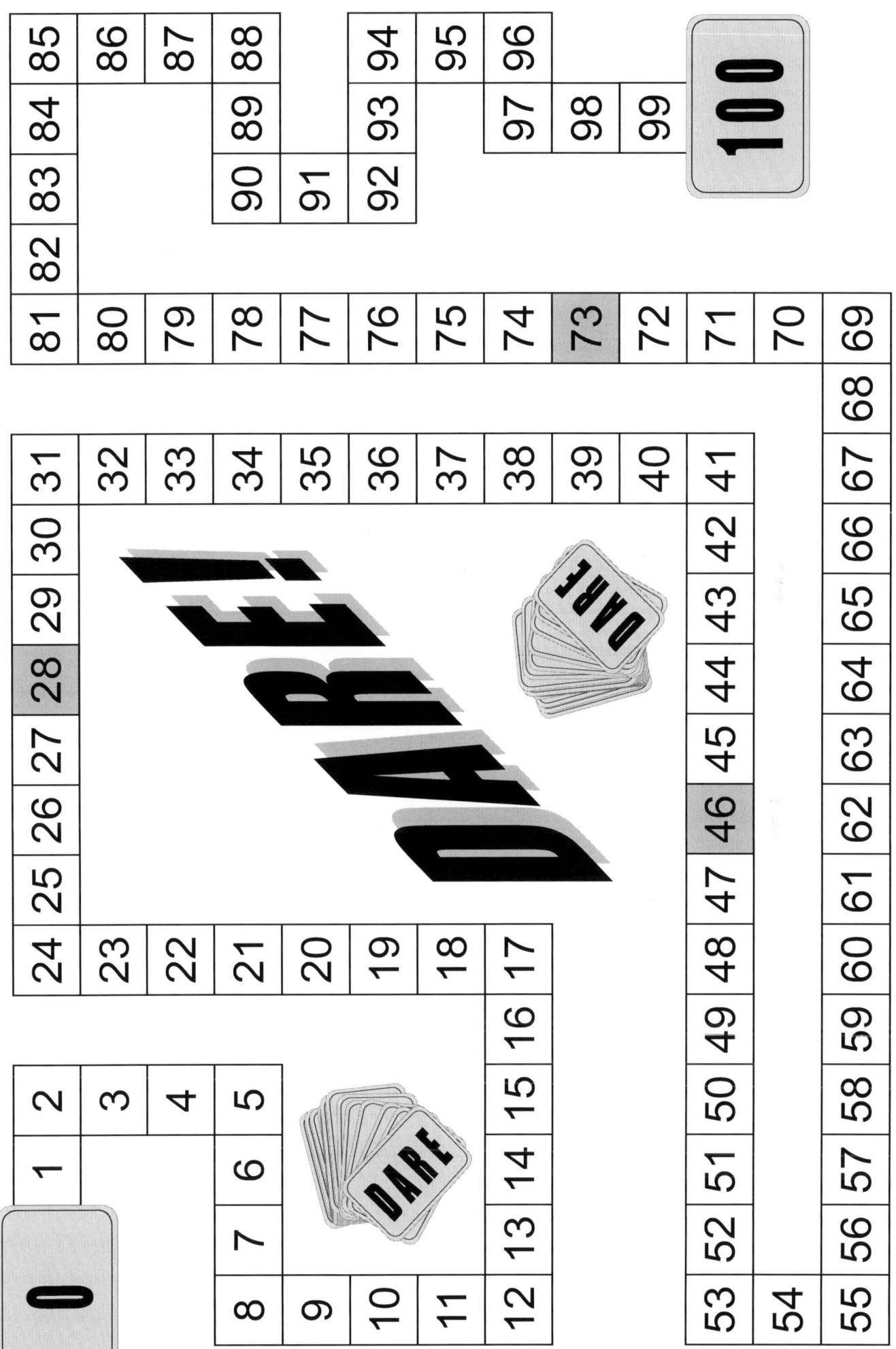

Speed Seekers

Focus

Speed Seekers is a game for two or more players which practices adding and subtracting one and two-digit numbers with some answers exceeding one hundred.

What you need

▶ Playing cards

▶ Counters (a different colour for each player)

▶ Speed Seekers game board

How to play

Firstly, the cards are shuffled and then placed in a pile, face-down and within reach of all the players. Player 1 takes a card from the top of the pack and doubles its value to get a total. They then subtract this total from eighty and move their counter on the board as shown in the diagram.

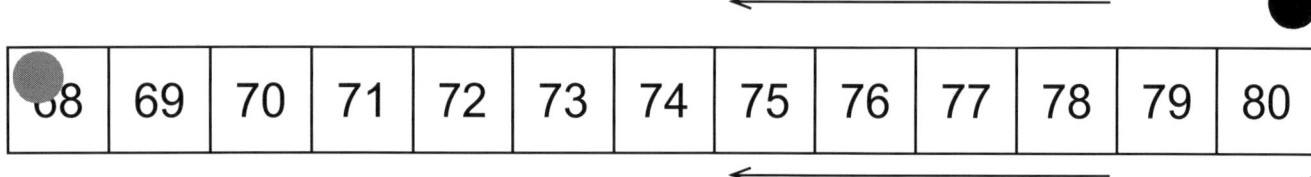

For example

Player 1 (grey counter) turns over a six. First of all they calculate double six (or 2 x 6 = 12). They then calculate 80 – 12 = 68 and move their counter to that position on the game board.

Play continues with players taking cards in turn, doubling them and then subtracting the total from the number underneath their counter on the game board.

▶ Players must do all their mental calculations before moving their counter. The player must also give the correct answer to move their counter otherwise it remains where it is on the game board.

▶ If a player lands on a Speed Seeker square they can choose to either move another nine spaces or move any one other player backwards nine squares on the game board.

▶ If a player lands on top of another counter, the counter landed on is moved back to the first Speed Seeker square they reach by moving backwards along the game board.

How to win

The first player to land on or go past zero (the finish line) on the game board is the winner.

Rule changes / Next steps

▶ The higher/lower cards can be removed from the pack to alter the difficulty of calculations.

▶ For Speed Seekers 120 the cards above eight are removed from the pack, along with the sevens. The eights and cards from ace to six are kept in the pack. Players turn over two cards and must multiply them together before subtracting that total from the number under their counter. Players landing on a Speed Seeker square can choose to either move forward nineteen spaces or move any other player back nineteen squares on the game board.

▶ Play as an addition game, starting at zero and adding up to the finish line.

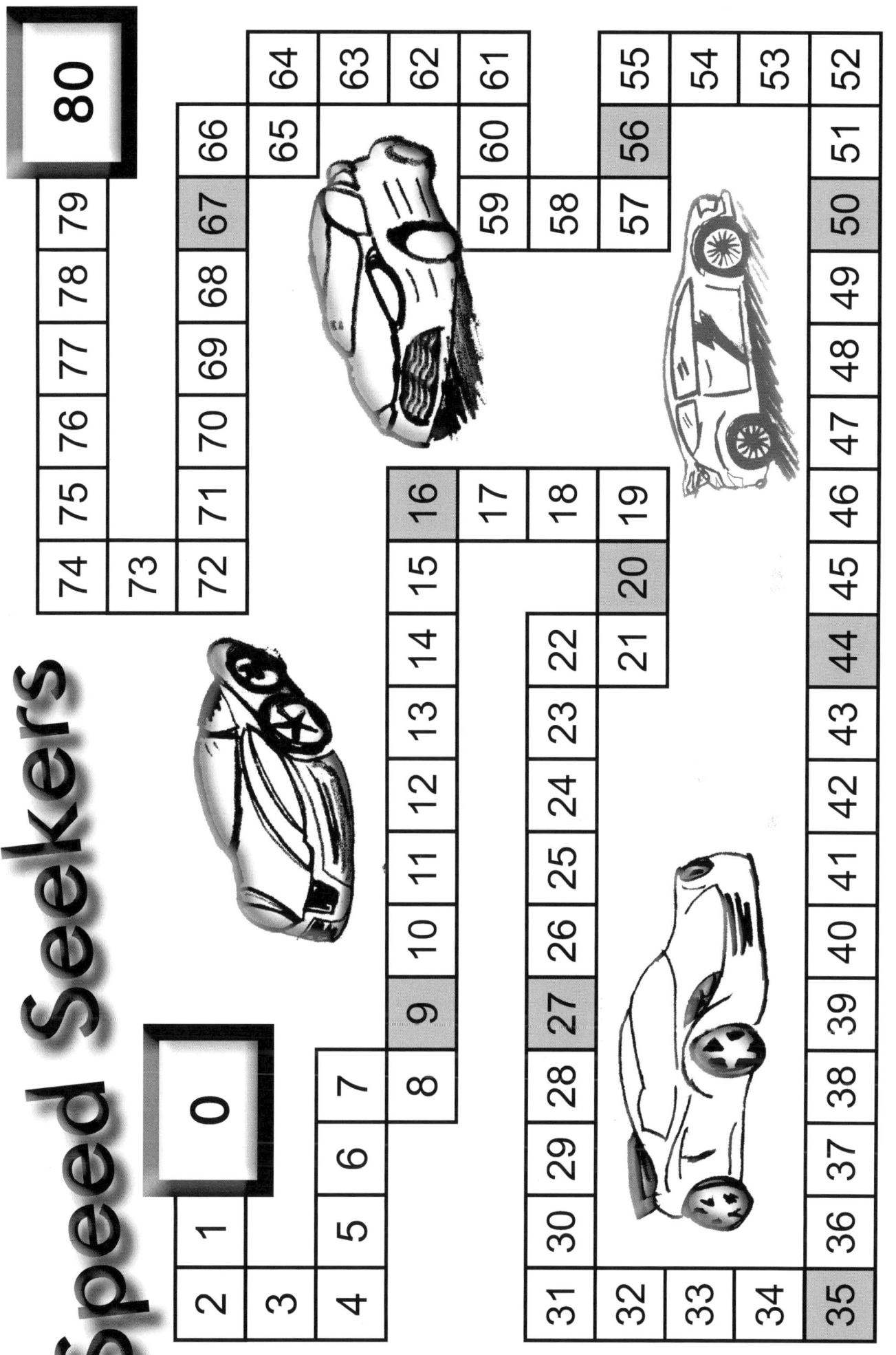

Speed Seekers

The Thousand Dash

Focus

The Thousand Dash is a game for two or more players which practices adding and subtracting three-digit numbers and tens with numbers up to one thousand.

What you need

▶ Playing cards

▶ Counters (a different colour for each player)

▶ The Thousand Dash game board

How to play

Firstly the cards are shuffled and then placed in a pile, face-down and within reach of all the players. Each player starts with a counter of their own colour at the start of the game board (first diagram).

Player 1 starts the game by turning over a card and placing it face-up in front of them. They multiply the number by ten and then move to that number on the game board.

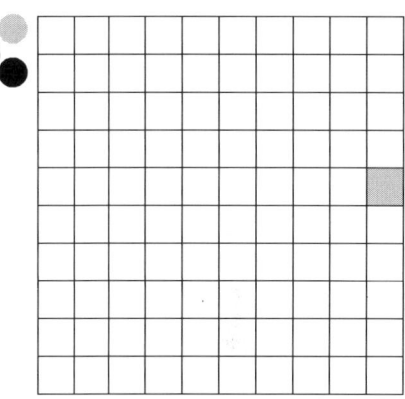

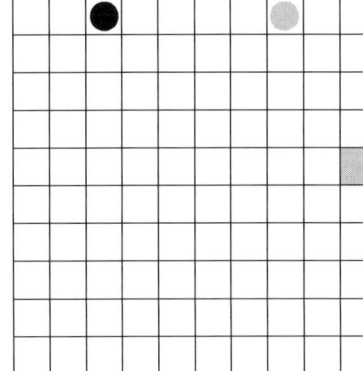

For example

Player 1 (black counter) turns over a three. This is multiplied by ten to make thirty (10 x 3 = 30) so Player 1 moves their counter to the matching number on the game board.

Player 2 (grey counter) then turns over an eight. This is multiplied by ten to make eighty (10 x 8 = 80), so Player 2 moves to that number on the board.

Play continues in this fashion. If, for example, Player 1 turned over a nine on their next turn they would have to do 30 + 90 = 120 and move to that position on the game board.

Players must do all their mental calculations before moving their counter. The player must also give the correct answer to move their counter, otherwise it remains in the same place on the game board.

If a player lands on top of another player's counter below five hundred they send their opponent back to the start. If the counter is beyond five hundred then it is sent back to that halfway square.

How to win

The first player to land on or go past a thousand (finish line) is the winner.

Rule changes / Next steps

▶ Start at a thousand, subtracting the value of the card multiplied by ten, with the finish line at zero.

▶ Players have a boost counter that they can play once in the game to double the number on their card. This could be played before or after the card is turned over.

▶ Encourage children to investigate patterns in adding and subtracting numbers, such as
15 – 6 = 9   so   150 – 60 = 90   and   1500 – 600 = 900.

The Thousand Dash

10	20	30	40	50	60	70	80	90	100
110	120	130	140	150	160	170	180	190	200
210	220	230	240	250	260	270	280	290	300
310	320	330	340	350	360	370	380	390	400
410	420	430	440	450	460	470	480	490	**500**
510	520	530	540	550	560	570	580	590	600
610	620	630	640	650	660	670	680	690	700
710	720	730	740	750	760	770	780	790	800
810	820	830	840	850	860	870	880	890	900
910	920	930	940	950	960	970	980	990	1000

Tower Power

Focus

Tower Power is a game for two or more players which can be used to practice a range of efficient mental methods with numbers up to twenty.

What you need

▶ Playing cards
▶ Counters

How to play

After shuffling the cards Player 1 deals out seven cards to each player and places the rest of the pack face-down and within reach of all the players.

As Player 1 dealt the cards, Player 2 goes first and must turn over a card from the top of the pack and place it face-up in clear view of everyone. All the players must then look at their cards and try to find ways of making the number on the card. Players can use any number of cards and any combination of addition, subtraction, multiplication and division.

For example
Player 1 turns over a queen. Players have to combine their cards to try and make twelve such as:

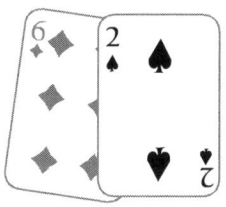
6 x 2 = 12

11 + 7 − 5 − 1 = 12

21 − 9 = 12

Players must place their combinations face-up in front of them for everyone to see and check that they are correct. Each player is allowed to place down as many combinations as they can, as long as they make twelve, but can only use each card once. They can then take a counter for each correct calculation they make and use them to start building a tower. After about half a minute to a minute players pick up all their cards so they still have the same seven cards in their hand for the next turn.

If a player can't find any ways of making the target number they can choose to change any one or two cards from their hand with one or two from the top of the pile. Play continues until a player turns over a number that has already been turned. All the cards are then collected from the players, shuffled, and Player 2 this time deals seven cards for the game to continue, with Player 3 turning the first card.

How to win

The first player to power up their tower to ten counters is the winner.

Rule changes / Next steps

▶ Play using only addition and subtraction.
▶ Double the number on each card turned to make higher target numbers.
▶ Use these calculations to show how the equals sign can be used to indicate equivalence, such as 6 x 2 = 11 + 1 = 12.

Trios

Focus

Trios is a game for four to six players which can be used to practice a range of efficient mental methods with numbers up to one hundred.

What you need

▶ Playing cards
▶ Counters (a different colour for each player)
▶ Trio game board

How to play

Player 1 turns over any number of cards and could be asked to add, subtract or multiply them to get an answer depending on what skill or knowledge from the Year 3 programme of study the game is being used to practice. If the player gets the answer correct they can place a counter of their own colour in a circle on the game board.

Player 2 then turns over one or more cards and performs a similar calculation. Play continues in this way with players taking it in turns to take one or more cards, answer questions and place counters on the game board. If a player gives an incorrect answer, they are unable to place a counter on that turn.

How to win

The first player to make a Trio is the winner. Trios can either be in a triangle or in a straight line as shown in the diagram.

Remove all the counters and play again.

Rule changes / Next steps

▶ Players continue to try and make Trios until all the spaces are covered or until the players agree that no more can be made. Players score three points for every Trio they make and the winner is the player with the most points at the end of the game.

▶ Restrict players to making only triangles or straight lines to win the game rather than allowing both.

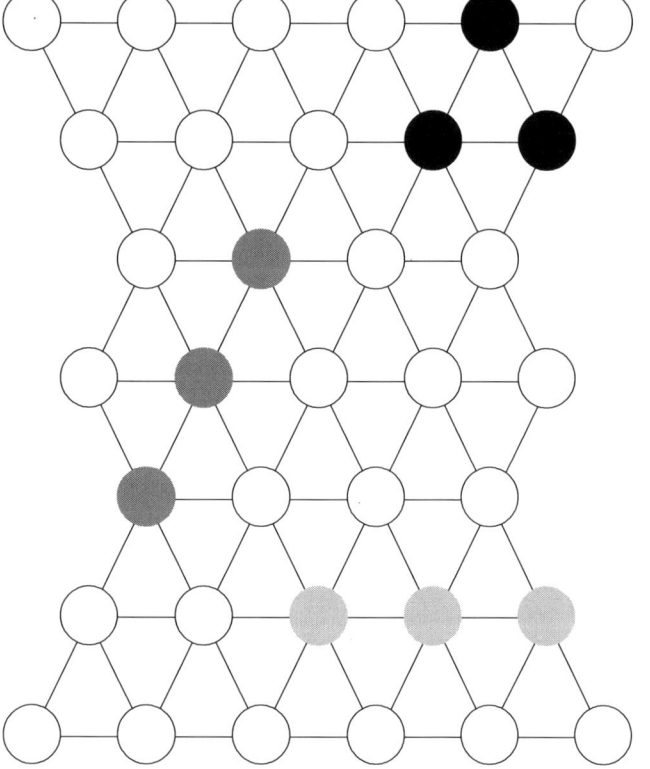

TRIOS

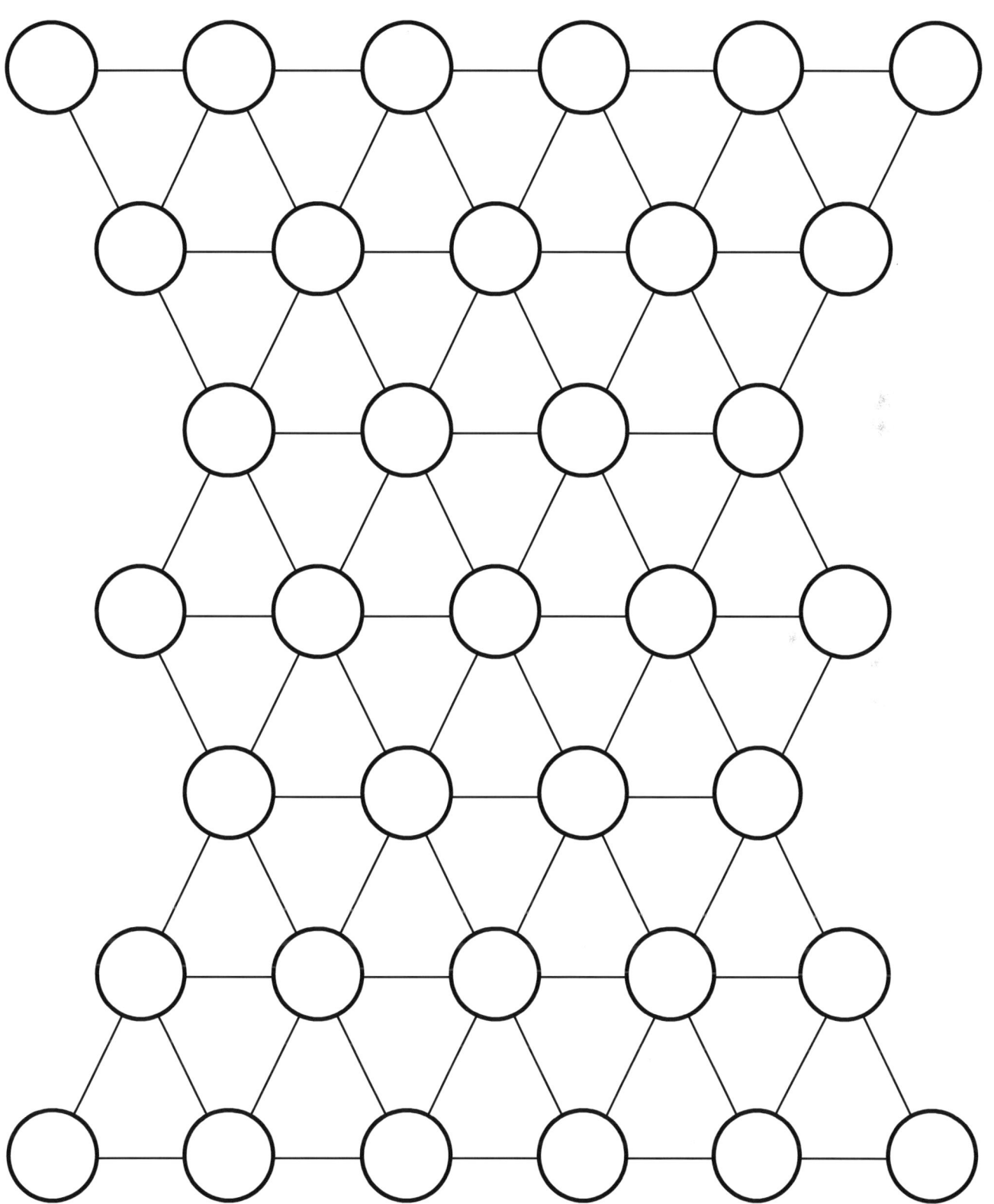

Monster Mash-Up

Focus

Monster Mash-up is a game for two to six players which can be used to practice a range of efficient mental methods with numbers up to one thousand.

What you need

▶ Playing cards (cards 1–5)

▶ Counters (one for each player)

▶ Monster Mash-Up game board

▶ Question cards, if using (see Next Steps, below)

How to play

When the cards from six upwards have been removed from the pack the remaining cards are shuffled and placed in a pile, face-down and within reach of all the players. Players then choose a monster and place their counter on it, ready for the start of the game.

Player 1 is asked a question by the question master to practice recall of facts or any skill within the Year 3 programme of study. If answered correctly Player 1 turns over a card and can then move the same number of spaces on the game board. If the answer is incorrect the player is not allowed to move their counter. The other players are then asked questions in turn. If correct they can turn over a card and move the same number of spaces on the game board.

Players must try and avoid the black holes in various positions on the game board, since landing on one sends them back to 'their' monster at the start of the game.

Players are allowed to move between tracks and go anywhere on the board, though can't keep moving backwards and forwards from one square to another.

If a player lands on top of another counter, the counter landed on is moved back to any monster of that player's choosing.

How to win

The first player to land on or go beyond an end square is the winner.

Rule changes / Next steps

▶ Players can move one bonus square if they can answer a question that another player has answered incorrectly.

▶ Different kinds of question may be selected, dependent, for example, on what a particular child needs to practice, or on particular skills needed for assessment purposes.

▶ Players must turn the exact number to land on an end square and win the game.

▶ Use the set of mixed mental questions provided. Put them face-down on the table for children to pick at random, read aloud and then answer. Alternatively, pass them to an appointed question master to read out.

What two numbers come next? 12, 16, 24, 28, ... , ...	What two numbers come next? 96, 88, 80, 72, ... , ...	What is 10 more than 274?	What is ten less than 517?
What is 100 more than 861?	What is 100 less than 135?	What is the 3 worth in 9<u>3</u>8?	What is the value of the underlined digit in 4<u>2</u>9?
True or False 366 > 345	True or False 808 < 792	Write the number three hundred and seven in figures.	Write the number six hundred and ninety in figures.
285 = 200 + __ + 5	146 = 130 + __	Take three tens away from 400.	Take six hundreds away from 1000.
What is 7 more than 128?	What is 9 less than 362?	Add 60 to 517.	Subtract 90 from 420.
354 + 400 =	903 − 800 =	76 + 17 =	64 − 16
43 + 75	109 − 22	17 = __ + 9	15 = 22 − __
__ + 30 = 210	__ − 20 = 41	What is the sum of 28 and 53?	What is the difference between of 78 and 83?

3 x 7 =	6 x 8 =	5 x 4 =	12 x 3 =
8 x 9 =	4 x 11 =	40 ÷ 5 =	18 ÷ 3 =
How many lots of 4 are there in 16?	How many groups of 8 can you make from 64?	If 4 x 3 = 12, what is 40 x 3	If 2 x 8 = 16, what is 20 x 8?
8 = __ x 2	__ ÷ 5 = 3	8 = 32 ÷ __	3 x __ = 27
What is ½ of 24?	What is ½ of 50?	Half a number is 7. What's the number?	I think of a number and halve it. The answer is 11. What's the number?
True or False? ⅛ > ¼	True or False? ⅓ < ½	What is ⅓ + ⅔?	What is ⅛ + ⅝?
What is ¼ of 12?	What is ¼ of 40?	What is ⅝ – ⅜?	What is ¾ – ¼?
What two numbers come next? 0, 0.1, 0.2, 0.3, … , …	What two numbers come next? 1.1, 1, 0.9, 0.8, … , …	Name another fraction which is equivalent to ½. Explain how you know.	How many halves are there in four whole ones?

Tarquin Mathematics Resources

Tarquin has more than a thousand product lines to support and enrich mathematics. You can browse them at **www.tarquingroup.com**.

To make it easy to buy what you need to really use this book, we have some special packages online — put the keyword ACE into the quick search box to see the full range at once.

- Packs of Playing Cards
- Coloured Counters
- Beads

Other Tarquin Products designed for you

Books

First Tables Colouring Book

Second Tables Colouring Book

Arithmetic Arithmetic

Mathematical Vocabulary 1

 and many, many more ...

Posters

One Million Poster

Multiples Poster

Equal Parts Poster

 and many, many more ...

Tarquin, Suite 74, 17 Holywell Hill, St Albans, AL1 1DT
Tel: +44 (0)1727833866 Fax: +44 (0)845 456 6385
www.tarquingroup.com Follow us on Twitter @TarquinGroup

Printed and bound by CPI Group (UK) Ltd, Croydon, CR0 4YY
20/03/2026
02075617-0001